Sark S

Jan Guy & Sue ...

Small Island Publishing — Sark

Cover - Les Laches & Creux Harbour

Published in 2011 by
Small Island Publishing
Sark, Channel Islands
GY10 1SF

www.smallislandpublishing.sark.gg

Text © Jan Guy
Images & design © Sue Daly
Maps copyright © States of Guernsey 2011

ISBN 978-0-9567396-1-2

Sark Strolls

～☙ Introduction ☙～

Sark is a place of adventure: dramatic cliffs, hidden coves, caves to explore, truly the stuff of 'Boys' Own' annuals. This book, though, will allow you to see the best of our tiny island by doing some fairly gentle walks. It is written by an old age pensioner, albeit a reasonably fit one, who loves the grandeur and beauty of Sark but doesn't believe in over exertion or walking for walking's sake. If you are feeling energetic though then Sark is a relatively small island so you might choose to join up two or three of the walks or, if you really have your 'seven league boots' on then you may even elect to do the whole lot in one go.

All the walks can be achieved in strong walking shoes and trainers are suitable for most of them in the summer. Wear what you find comfortable but carry a light waterproof and a drink in your pack because Sark can easily offer a downpour and really hot sun within the space of ten minutes! I find shorts comfortable to walk in but occasionally one can encounter stinging nettles.

Dixcart Woods

The **time** it takes to do the walk rather than the **distance covered** is given and this is also how island signs give information. The starting point of each walk is indicated with a star on the map. The times given in the book refer to a fairly leisurely walking pace with plenty time to take in the view, enjoy the smell of the flowers, or appreciate the soaring and diving of a peregrine falcon. Sark is better not taken in haste.

The walks are of varying length and over varying terrain. Sark is a plateau some 100 metres (300 feet) above sea level so paths down to the sea involve some descending and the inevitable ascending to get back. Some walks skirt the edges of fields. Most involve some road walking but what we call roads you would probably call cart tracks though do remember Sark does have tractors, horse drawn vehicles and bicycles sharing the roads with you. As well as outlining the routes, view points and things of particular interest are mentioned and often pictured. Wildlife of particular interest also gets a mention though it varies throughout the season, of course.

My walks often involve a swim or a picnic along the way. The sea is chilly, rarely more than 18 degrees centigrade, but wonderfully clean, clear and refreshing and it is oh so lovely to come out into the sun after! There are many benches, mostly donated by visitors in memory of a loved one who had happy times in Sark, and the odd picnic table but generally your lunch can be taken where you will: next to the path, on the beach or on a warm rock overlooking the sea.

Most of the paths are managed by the Island's Public Work department and work on them is usually carried out by just one operator. In general though the land over which you will walk is not owned by the Island but access is permitted by the owners and obviously care and consideration are appreciated. Occasionally paths are closed but if you are carrying the Sark Tourist Map, available free from which ever shipping company you travel with and from the Island's Official Tourism Office, the Visitor Centre, next to the Prison, it is easy to reroute with out adding much to the distance.

The west coast

❧ The Coastal Code ❧

• For your own safety, keep to the paths and the roads. You explore Sark at your own risk.

• Dogs are welcome under close supervision as long as you are not walking through fields with livestock in. Please clear up after your pet and never let them chase birds.

• Cliffs and grassland are vulnerable to fire. Please don't light fires or discard lighted cigarettes.

• Enjoy the wildflowers but don't pick them. Help marine creatures by turning rocks back to their original position when exploring the seashore and always keep an eye on the tide.

• Love Sark and please take your litter home or use the bins.

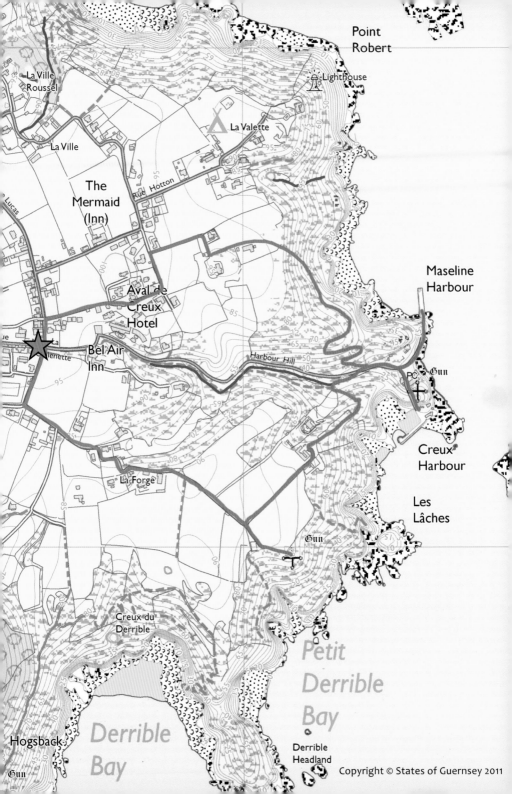

Point
Robert

Lighthouse

La Ville
Roussel

La Valette

La Ville

Rue Hotton

The
Mermaid
(Inn)

Maseline
Harbour

Aval de
Creux
Hotel

Bel Air
Inn

Harbour Hill

PC
Gun

Gun

Creux
Harbour

La Forge

Les
Lâches

Gun

Petit
Derrible
Bay

Creux du
Derrible

Hogsback

Derrible
Bay

Derrible
Headland

Gun

Walk One
The South East

The walk, which starts and ends at La Colinette, takes about an hour and a half, a little more if you decide to explore, or swim in, Creux Harbour. The terrain is predominantly road and paths with a little field walking. There is a fairly steep ascent about half way through the walk. There are public toilets and a café at the harbour also about half way through the walk.

Walk south down the road from La Colinette with the Nat West Bank on your right. Follow the road down hill. At La Peigneurie ignore signs to Dixcart Bay on the right and continue on the road, around several bends and passing La Vieille Forge.

Cannon at Les Laches

At the brow of the hill, follow signs to Les Laches continuing on the road.

At the next junction, bear left, signed 'To the Harbour', but first you may prefer to take a brief detour to the cannon and radio mast which you can see ahead. The cannon was made in Falkirk between 1795 and 1798 and given to the island to assist in defence. The radio mast is to enhance VHF radio used by shipping. From this point you enjoy outstanding views over Jersey, with the infamous Paternoster Reef in front of the north coast of that island and you can look down in to Creux Harbour on your left.

Creux Harbour

Les Burons

If you have enjoyed the detour, return to the junction signed 'To the Harbour'. Continue down that road crossing the grass at a small stand of pines after about 300 metres to join a grassy path signed 'To Harbours'. Descend this path noting the strong tidal flow at both high and low water between Sark and the off lying rocks called Les Burons. You may even be fortunate enough to glimpse common or bottle-nosed dolphins playing in the current, especially near high water.

Common Dolphins

Continue on this path, descending shallow steps. Just before you reach the road (Harbour Hill) turn right on the path which continues parallel to the road. Where it joins the road, cross Harbour Hill to join a path signed 'Cliff Path'.

If, at this point, you feel the need for a swim, refreshment or a loo stop instead of crossing the road go down it to the harbour area. Sark's harbours are vital to island life. Everything that comes here has to come by boat: most food, building materials, coal, oil and of course, people. All cargo has to be craned off the boat and transported by tractor and trailer up to the top of the island. A lovely swim can be enjoyed from the beach at the top of Creux Harbour, often referred to as the Old Harbour, from half tide up to half tide down. The drying harbour of Creux is a good example of 'perfect in miniature'. Built of granite blocks, some of them from Jersey, it was originally used as a harbour by the Jersey settlers in 1588, though it was very different from the harbour that you see now. You can still make out that date in the stone above the old tunnel next to the café on the seaward side.

Creux Harbour

It was improved over the years. The south arm was added for more protection and the gap, where the present hardstanding is, was filled in. It was used for the film set of Toilers of the Sea in the 1930s. The harbour has one disadvantage though: it is dry or shallow for about half the tidal cycle. As tourism increased, ferrying passengers ashore in small boats for part of the time was no longer acceptable. As a result the less attractive, but more functional, Maseline Jetty was completed in 1949. This allows access at all states of the tide but in strong north east winds it is not good and tiny Creux is then still used for both ferries and cargo boats from Guernsey when the tide is in.

The 'toast rack' Harbour Hill transport

If you have used up all your energy and can't face more walking then wait for the tractor bus which meets every scheduled boat and will take you back to the Collinette for a small charge. Alternatively, shorten the walk by using the footpath which runs parallel to Harbour Hill up the left hand side.

Harbour Hill footpath

Maseline Harbour

If you wish to continue the walk, return to the path signed 'Cliff Path'. As you ascend zig zag fashion and gain more height views over La Grande Moie, a rock which is an early summer breeding ground for razorbills, Alderney and, over to the left of Alderney, the Casquets light open out and you can look down into Maseline Harbour, perhaps busy with passengers or cargo handling.

La Grande Moie

Towards the end of the path there is a small block enclosure. This was where Malcolm Robson, renowned yachtsman, Sark Pilot and founder of Sark power station used to observe what was going on out at sea. Ascend up to the gate. Go through and bear left. The path opens on to a field and you need to walk along the left hand side of this. At the end of the field turn right along the road and at the T junction bear left. After about 100 metres there is a gap in the hedge and a drain grate beneath your feet. Go through the gap and continue between a group of modern houses and then along a small road until you come to a T junction. Bear left to get back to La Colinette.

Génétière

a Couteur

La Ville
Roussel
de Bas

*La Grève
de la
Ville*

Gulls
Chapel

Point
Robe

Lighthouse

La Ville
Roussel

La Valette

La Ville

Rue Lucas

Rue Hotton

The
Mermaid
(Inn)

Aval de
Creux
Hotel

The Avenue

La
Venette

Bel Air
Inn

Harbour Hill

La Forge

⚛ Walk Two ⚛
The East

The walk, which takes about forty minutes but at least an additional forty if you decide to descend to Grève de la Ville, is an easy stroll involving roads and some field walking and begins at La Colinette. The descent to Grève de La Ville, however, adds a more demanding dimension with a steep, though not particularly difficult, descent and ascent. The best time to enjoy this stroll is in the morning.

Point Robert

Walk north from La Colinette leaving the HSBC Bank on your right. Take the second turn on the right, pass the Mermaid Tavern on your left. At the next junction go left then almost immediately right with an attractive stone house on your left making the corner. Descend the hill. At the bottom bear left then almost immediately right up a concrete track signed 'Lighthouse closed. Viewing point only'. This brings you above Point Robert Lighthouse. It is no longer manned so you can only visit by special arrangement but you will get a very good view passing close beneath it if you are returning on the boat to Guernsey. Point Robert Lighthouse was completed in 1913. This Trinity House Lighthouse warns shipping away from the many off lying rocks around the east coast of Sark. The light signal can be seen from 20 miles away and there is also a high pitched fog signal.

The lighthouse was popular with duty keepers. Though classified as a rock station, and therefore well paid, its obvious connection to Sark meant that it was perhaps the only rock station from whence the keepers could visit the pub during their off duty hours! However, like many other lighthouses, in 1993 the lighthouse was automated and the keepers left. Enjoy the views of a rock called La Grande Moie, home of breeding razorbills, guillemots, gulls and shags, with the Normandy coast just 25 miles away and Alderney and the Casquets to the north.

Bear left just before the wall and skirt the field until you come to a gap. Continue with the hedge on your right until you reach a narrow gap with a stone stile. Go over the stile and proceed diagonally across the field. Follow the path on the right around the cliff but go through a small gate on your left about 50 metres before the end of the path then follow the path between two fields. Where the field joins the road, turn right.

If you feel the need for a swim follow the sign on your right to Grève de la Ville. The zig zag path descends quite steeply and the swimming from this pebbly cove is best from about half tide up to half tide down, ideally in the morning when you can dry off in the sun. Even if you don't go right the way down, it is worth finding the bench at the first turning just to experience the peace and the view but if you want coffee you will have to have your flask. No cafes or pubs here.

Grève de la Ville & the Gulls' Chapel

To rejoin the walk go back to the sign and bear right on the road. Pass La Ville Farm, a very fine example of a Guernsey style farm house. Completed in 1701 it has recently been very sympathetically restored.

La Ville Farm

At the crossroad bear left then left again at the next one to return to La Colinette, stopping, perhaps, at Sark's Occupation and Heritage Museum on the way to learn a little more of the island's history.

Occupation & Heritage Museum

Béc du
Nez

La Grune

Congrière

Boutiques
Caves

Butts

Eperquerie
(landing)

Le Platon

Gun

Fortifications

Les
Fontaines

Guillaumesse

Creux
Belet

Le Grand
Creux

Les Sept
Moies

Le Fort

aignie

Bay

Les
Autelets

La G

Clos de
Camps

La C

tte
ck

Window in
the Rock

L'Ecluse

La Seigneurie

La Râde
Copyright © States of Guernsey 2011

∾ Walk Three ∾
L'Eperquerie

L'Eperquerie, although sometimes referred to as L'Eperquerie Common is not common land in the English sense of the word. This wonderfully wild area on the north of the island is made up of land owned by several tenants and one can stroll as much, or as little, as one pleases. This walk, which takes about an hour and is not too demanding though there is a little descending and ascending, gives a very good sample of all the Eperquerie has to offer. In spring and early summer the area is golden with coconut-scented gorse while an autumn walk and picnic can be supplemented by blackberries picked en route. This is also one of the best areas in Sark for glimpsing the secretive Dartford warbler which breeds here. There are a number of benches and other picnic spots with a wide variety of views, perhaps some of the best that Sark has to offer. There is a swim option from the pebbly cove at L'Eperquerie landing (half tide up to half tide down) and the snorkelling is good there too. If you just wish to dip your toes in seawater and the tide is low try the Eperquerie Pool.

L'Eperquerie Landing

The walk starts on the road which goes past La Seigneurie at a point where there is a sign saying 'L'Eperquerie and Shooting Range'. Follow the sign to L'Eperquerie. Where the road stops enjoy views over Cap de La Hague on the French Coast to the east, Alderney and the Casquets to the north, a black and white day mark for shipping called the Grande Amfroque and a rocky area called the Humps, a seabird breeding sanctuary to the north west. Herm and its long strand of Shell Beach lie to the west with Guernsey behind it.

View across to Herm & Shell Beach

Walk straight down the path (rather than left or right) leaving the litter bin on your left. In a short time, the path joins a wider track where you bear left. Ignore the grassy paths on your right proceeding along the main track. Where the path forks bear right signed 'L'Eperquerie Landing and Fontaines Bay'. To go down to the landing and the pool bear right just before the cannon and follow a winding path through the gap in an ancient wall right down to the beach.

From this beach, small fishing boats used to be launched and close examination reveals the remains of a slipway and rings in some of the rocks. The pool was concreted between the wars so that it would retain water and could be used as a play pool for children. It is still popular and when a wall collapsed it was recently restored by members of La Société Sercquaise, the island's local history and natural history society.

L'Eperquerie gateway

L'Eperquerie paddling pool

To resume the walk go back to the cannon. This one was made in Falkirk between 1795 and 1798 and is mounted on oak from trees uprooted in the 1987 gale which did considerable damage in Sark. Do not ascend on the main path but descend on the path which starts between the cannon and the bench. Continue along the grassy path, perhaps observing the ferry from Guernsey negotiating the tricky inside passage between the rock called La Pecheresse and the land.

Bon Marin heading for Maseline Harbour

Bec du Nez

At the next junction bear left and upwards. At this point there is an option to walk further north to view a carving that was carried out by a group of Buddhist monks in 2000. To do this keep straight on then right towards a tower which is slightly off to the left. Pass over a very narrow section of the path. On your left at this point is the scramble down to the entrance to the Boutiques, a cave system that should only be explored with local advice and a good knowledge of tides. If you want to view the carving from the tower, bear left and left again. Stand with your back to the tower and look north for a large block of rock with intricate carvings. If you wish to get right up to the rock do not take the two left turnings, just keep on the lower path. It is interesting to note how the carving is already eroding, witness to the wild weather that our island can experience. There is a bench by the carved stone. To return to the main walk retrace your steps.

Buddhist carving

You are now facing Brecqhou with its modern castle. Down on your right is an isolated rock called Guillaumesse which boasts an underwater nature trail which can be enjoyed by experienced divers. Continue on this path ignoring all paths to the left and right. After a slight change of level, bear right but ignore the next right and proceed on the main path. After about two hundred metres you may notice a rounded stone saying 'Beth Hurden 1921 to 1996'. Though American by birth, Beth lived on Sark for many years and loved the natural beauty of the island. Behind the memorial and the bigger stones which surround it is a bench and it is worth spending a few moments there to reflect and enjoy the view. The sea stacks on your left are called Les Autelets and, in late spring and early summer, are home to the largest guillemot colony in the Channel Islands. The Gouliot Passage is the narrow gap between Sark and Brecqhou and tides there can run at up to ten knots at high and low tide creating huge waves when wind and tides are against each other. The

Cannon on L'Eperquerie Common

Sark side of this area, the Gouliot Headland, has been designated a Ramsar site because of the very special sea caves and their surrounds. (See walk 5). Proceed along the main path leaving the next bench on your right to regain the road. Bear right to return to your starting point.

The west coast & Les Autelets

Saignie
Bay

Les
Autelets

Clos de
Camps

L'Ecluse

La Seigneurie

La Râde

Window in
the Rock

La Moinerie
Hotel

Prise de
Bercevil

La Rondellerie

Island
Hall

Le Port

Mont Plaisir Road

Hotel
Petit
Champs

Copyright © States of Guernsey 2011

❧ Walk Four ❧
Port du Moulin

This walk, which takes in some of the most interesting areas of the island, is on varied terrain and, if you choose to go right down to the pebbly beach, includes one fairly steep descent and ascent. Walking fairly gently, the route, which starts and ends outside the main gate of La Seigneurie, takes about an hour and a half but allow another thirty minutes if you wish to explore the bay.

Port du Moulin & Les Autelets

Walk north leaving the elaborate commemorative garden gates on your left. Take the first turning on your left, signed 'Window in the Rock and Port du Moulin'. After Maison Rouge Gallery on your left and a bike park on your right go straight on at the next junction signed 'Window in the Rock and Port du Moulin'.

When you come to the next junction on this path the walk proper requires you to turn left, signed to 'Window in the Rock and Port du Moulin' but in late spring and early summer a very special option to precede your walk is to carry straight on along the path with honeysuckle and blackthorn on each side until you come to a gap on your left. The few steps down to the barrier will leave you standing above Les Autelets, sea stacks the French name of which means 'The Altars'. The largest of the stacks is the breeding site of the biggest guillemot colony in the Channel Islands and this addition to the walk allows an outstanding view of these beautiful avian visitors to the island.

Guillemots on their breeding ledges

The birds arrive in spring after spending winter far out to sea. Each pair lays a single egg relying on its pointed shape to prevent it from rolling off the ledge as they build no nest at all. Three weeks or so after hatching the chicks half flutter and half tumble into the sea at dusk where their fathers lure them away from land and predatory gulls. The males spend up to six weeks teaching the young birds how to dive for fish and by the middle of July all of the guillemots have returned to the open sea. The detour to see the guillemot colony is on a private path which does not allow entry through the gate at the far end so you need to walk back the way you came to rejoin the main walk. (Cyclists are reminded that bikes must be left in the bike park.)

Guillemot

View through Window in the Rock

Returning to the junction mentioned before, start your descent in to the valley on a zig zag path and continue down this path. This area is called L'Ecluse (the lock or, in this case, sluice) and the cove below is Port du Moulin (the Port of the Mill). These may seem rather incongruous names but in Sark's monastic era there was a water mill, or possibly more than one, on the stream on your left.

Heeding the warning signs, carry on down to the well-named 'Window in the Rock'. Not a natural feature, this hole was blasted out on the directions of Seigneur William Thomas Collings when, in the 1850s, the potential for Sark as a tourist destination began to be realised. The view over Les Autelets and the north west coast is surely a romantic's dream, as long as he or she has a head for heights! Leave with your back to the Window and then branch right. The machinery that is left on the ground is all that remains of a hoist, used for bringing up seaweed, a wonderful natural fertiliser, from the bay.

Port du Moulin

Retrace your steps and take the first turning on your right to go down to the bay. This is a perfect place for swimming from around half tide up to half tide down. The water is wonderfully clear and the snorkelling very good. At low tide it is possible to venture through the rock arch, scene of the descent of Miss George in the television adaptation of Mervyn Peake's 'Mr Pye', (though she did not start from the top. Another location on L' Eperquerie was utilised for that). Though the rocks beneath the arch are slippery, if you proceed a little way you may catch a glimpse of the metal ribs and other components of a ship. This was not an accidental wreck. In 1938 a film was made of Victor Hugo's 'Toilers of the Sea' and Les Autelets stood in for the Roches-Douvres. The ship was placed in the area to represent the shipwreck which is essential to the plot.

Wreckage at Les Autelets

On completion of your exploration of the cove, ascend to just beyond the window in the rock and cross the stream. Turn right to experience another fabulous viewpoint and a couple of, perhaps rather welcome, benches but to continue the walk turn left after crossing and ascend the valley on the other side. Continue on this path as it bends right and at the junction of paths bear right. At the next junction turn right admiring grand views over Jethou, Herm and Guernsey. As the view of Brecqhou opens up turn left then left then right in rapid succession. Continue along this path with a wall on your left. At the junction with a track turn right then immediately left. Follow this track until you reach a junction with a large house on your right. Turn left, walking under conifers. Enter a vineyard through a black metal gate. Vines are a new venture for Sark and much research has been done which suggests that the island will be able to produce good quality wine in future years. Bear right on a wide track and then left. At the next junction bear diagonally right walking with vines on either side.

At the end of the vines go through the gate and carry straight on to join the Seigneurie Road at which you turn left to return to the starting point.

Vines

Moulin

L'Ecluse

Window in
the Rock

Tintageu

Pegane

La
H

Prise de
Bercevil

Port à la
Jument

Moie du
Mouton

Le Port

Saut à
Juan

Hotel
Petit
Champs

RAMSAR
Site

Gouliot
Caves

Le Petit
Beauregard

La Vaurocqu

Gouliot
Headland

Havre
osselin

Le Grand
Beauregard
(demolished)

Landing

La Fregondée

Pilcher
Monument

Victor
Hugo Cave

Moie des
Orgeries

Port ès
Saies

Plaisa

✒ Walk Five ✒
The Gouliot Headland

The Gouliot Headland is a Ramsar Site, recognised world wide as having special animal and plant life, particularly the marine life in the Gouliot Caves, a large sea cave system on the Sark side of the Gouliot Passage. The walk described here does not take in the caves, which are quite a clamber and require a good knowledge of tides, but does allow you to experience the wild and wide open feeling of this dramatic area. The walk is on easy terrain: roads, tracks and grass paths and is at its best in late April and early May when the area is covered, quite literally, in bluebells and primroses. Botanists may also spot one or two white bluebells (not to be confused with the common wild garlic) and the tiny, delicate and rare sand crocus which grow there in early spring. (See the wildflower guide on pages 72 and 73) The walk, which takes about 45 minutes and starts at the Methodist Chapel, is also a delightful evening walk in summer, a sunset walk, perhaps after an early dinner. As the area is frequently grazed by livestock please take care to close the several gates through which you will pass.

Port à la Jument House

With your back to the Chapel, follow the minor road signed Port à la Jument and Petit Champ. Continue down this road for about ten minutes, admiring Port à la Jument house, a classic Jersey style farmhouse on your right.

The Gouliot Headland in spring with Jethou, Herm & Shell Beach in the distance

Also on your right there are grand views over Jethou and Herm, and even a bench to admire them from. At the entrance to Le Vieux Port bear left then right on a track signed Port à la Jument. (This is referring to the bay of that name, not the house which you have just passed.) Follow this track, noticing, on your right, Jaydn's Wood, a stand of young trees planted to celebrate the birth of a young Sarkee who is, at the time of writing, age ten.

The view looking north

Leaving a corrugated barn on your left and a stone barn on your right continue on the track signed Port à la Jument. Pass through the gate and skirt the field keeping on the right. You should see the finger-like obelisk of the Pilcher Monument in the distance, slightly off to the left. Go up to the next gate and pass through it bearing left on a wide grassy track going down towards the Island of Brecqhou. Pass through a gap in the bank with a bench on your left continuing on the grassy track bearing left towards the monument. The spur on your right is over the Gouliot Caves and it is well worth walking a little way down this to watch wheeling fulmars. The rocky outcrop on the top of the spur also offers one of the most wonderful picnic spots on the island: no benches, no picnic tables though, just amazing views over Brecqhou, or Little Sark or watch the wildness of the Gouliot Passage where the tide can run up to ten knots, giving huge standing waves if the wind is against the tide.

Continue on the main track as it bears left through two stone gate posts. (The gate is usually open). Shortly after the next gate, which you go through, you will join a road. Bear right, pass through the gate, then almost immediately bear left. Pass Le

Good Friday at Beauregard Pond

Petit Beauregard and the duck pond on your left. The pond is little used, except by the mallards and the moorhens, but on Good Friday morning there is a long tradition that the children of the island come out to sail their model boats while their parents hug mugs of hot chocolate and munch hot cross buns to support which ever charity the event organisers choose.

Continue on the road until you reach a T junction at which you turn left to return to the Methodist Chapel.

ᴈ A Little Bit About the Gouliot Caves ᴈ

The caves underwater

Soft Coral

Sponges

The Gouliot Caves are accessible by foot for a short time on the lowest spring tides. The scramble down the cliffs to sea level is only recommended for those with the surest of feet and a good head for heights and in the company of someone who knows the caves well.

The caves are open to the sea on both sides of the headland allowing up to ten knots of current to surge through the network of caverns on all but the lowest tides. The water is laden with plankton, the tiny plants and animals that form the basis of the food chain in the sea. As a result, every available surface of rock in the lower part of the caves is carpeted with marine life, much of which is normally only found in deeper water. As the tide falls the creatures are left out of water but the shaded walls of the caves stay damp and cool enough for the animals to survive until the water returns. The result is a colourful patchwork of marine life including sponges, anemones and even some corals. The most numerous anemones are the Beadlets which thrive by their thousands in shades of red, orange and green with 'beads' of electric blue beneath their tentacles. Jewel and Elegant Anemones also flourish and the intense colours of all of these creatures led the central section to be called the Jewel Cave.

For experienced divers the caves can be enjoyed underwater for about half an hour during the slack water around half tide when the true beauty of the caves is revealed. The anemones and corals unfurl their tentacles to feed and, on a sunny day, the walls are spotlit by shafts of bluey-green light filtering down from above.

The uniqueness of the caves, along with the wealth of marine life they support and the variety of flora above, led to the Gouliot Headland being declared a Wetland of International Importance under the Ramsar Convention in April 2007.

The Jewel Cave

ᨒᨑ Walk Six ᨑᨒ
La Coupée & the Pilcher Monument

This walk, which takes about two hours, allowing time to have a good look at both La Coupée and the Pilcher Monument, is over varied terrain: roads, paths and tracks some of which can be muddy in wet weather. There is a certain amount of change of level, some shallow steps and one stile. The walk starts and ends at the Visitor Centre which is at the western end of the Avenue, next to the tiny prison.

La Coupée

Turn left as you leave the Visitor Centre yard. Follow the road around the bend then turn left on a meadow path, signed 'Dixcart Hotel, Stocks Hotel, Dixcart Bay'. Descend down this path passing Stocks Hotel on your right. At the junction bear right then hard left walking on the road that passes Dixcart Hotel which will be on your left.

Stocks Hotel

These two hotels were the first to welcome staying visitors when tourism became popular in Sark. Victor Hugo was a regular at Dixcart while he resided in Guernsey and Stocks became a popular family hotel while W F Collings, the Dame of Sark's father, was Seigneur. Stocks was also temporary home to a large number of German soldiers billeted there in the Second World War.

Continue up the road until you come to a stile on your right, signed 'La Coupée'. Skirt the field with a wooden fence on your left. Enjoy distant views over Jersey. Cross the next stile and continue along a path, which winds and descends with some shallow steps to minimise slipping. In late summer and early autumn you will be able to sample a few blackberries to keep you going! The path starts to ascend and views over L' Étac and Little Sark open out. The low, long white building on Little Sark is called La Cloture de Bas but it is usually known as the Barracks as it housed miners during the silver mining bonanza. (See walk 9). Dixcart Bay is on the left below. The path continues, skirting a field on its seaward side. Just before the end of the field, bear left and go through the barrier, heeding warning signs, to get a bird's eye view of La Coupée or go through the gap at the end of the field and turn left to walk down to the isthmus. This is a busy area with many carriages and bikes so reasonable caution should be taken, especially on La Coupée itself.

La Coupée is a natural feature, 100 yards long and 260 feet high, joining Little and Big Sark. Erosion has always been an issue and in 1811 the width of the roadway was reduced to less than a stride. A retaining wall was built on the west after a fall in 1862 and in 1900 the first protecting rail was put up. This was improved, and a concrete roadway was built in 1945, by German prisoners of war working under Royal Engineers. A plaque to commemorate this can be seen on the left hand side in the centre of the isthmus. Erosion continues and you will see repairs that were carried out on the left hand (east) side in recent times. Sadly, in December 2009, a large landslip covered part of the path down to Grande Grève, the bay on the west side, preventing access to the beach at the time of writing.

Plaque commemorating the German POWs who worked on La Coupée in 1945

After a look at La Coupée, continue up the road passing the Chocolate Factory on your left and the hamlet of Dos D'Ane shortly after. At the junction with the road down to Stocks and Dixcart Hotels turn left on to a wide track. Go through a gate and continue along this bridle path, admiring views over Little Sark on the left. Shortly you will be looking over a valley on your left. This is known as Happy Valley and is particularly beautiful in years when the bluebells and primroses overlap in late spring. On these occasions the valley floor appears as a blue and pale yellow carpet. Happy Valley is also the most popular venue for sledging and skiing on the rare occasions when Sark has a significant fall of snow. Though it is no longer possible to descend to it, there is a beach called Port ès Saies at the end of the valley. Here, from a cave in the corner, some copper was mined at the time of the mining boom and, in more recent times, sand and gravel were taken commercially from the beach.

Happy Valley

Go through the next gate and, after about 150 metres, bear left to face tiny Beauregard cottage. This was recently rebuilt using the original stone and to the original design. The large flat area that you are now in was the site of Beauregard Hotel, built in the 1890s and recently demolished. There are plans to build a new hotel. Walk straight on with the cottage on your right and a traditional well on your left. Continue straight on with a modern stone faced house on your right and a bungalow on your left. Bear left at Hunter's Lodge and at the fork bear right walking towards the monument.

Beauregard Cottage

The plaques on the monument give you all the information that you need to know about the tragic shipwreck that the monument commemorates. Reverend Cachemaille, vicar and chronicler of Sark records that: "They were told not to go and that night would overtake them" and that evening departure on October 19th 1868 resulted in the deaths of all on board. Where the boat and the drowned men were found illustrates much about the vagaries of tidal currents. The gig was found near Dielette on the Normandy peninsula east of Sark, and bodies were found at Havre Gosselin (the small harbour below the monument), in the Gouliot Caves (just north of the monument) and at Niton in the Isle of Wight. Dr Gatehouse's body was never recovered at all.

The area around the monument is one of the very few places in the archipelago of the Channel Islands from which all the islands can be seen: Jersey can be glimpsed beyond La Coupée on the left, Alderney by looking north (behind you as you face the smaller plaque on the monument), Brecqhou close ahead, then Herm and Jethou with Guernsey behind them. To the north you can see some of the caves in the Gouliot Headland for which this area is well known. (See walk five.)

Havre Gosselin

The Mill

Go a little way down the path on the right of the monument (as you face out to sea) to view Havre Gosselin. This natural harbour is very popular with visiting yachtsmen. If you really feel the need for a swim, take the path all the way down to the tiny breakwater and use it as a launching platform but this is not advised when there is even a small swell.

To return to the Visitor Centre retrace your steps to join the road. Pass Beauregard Cottage on your right. At the next junction take the right turn, passing the duck pond on your left. Ignore the next track which turns off to the right. At the T junction turn right then immediately left, signed "Village, Harbour". Pass the tower of a mill on your right.

This mill was completed in 1571 by the de Carteret settlers and the Seigneur held a monopoly over milling rights, though this was challenged a number of times over the centuries. A third storey was added in 1797 when Seigneur Le Pelley was obliged to modernise after a fire. The mill fell in to disrepair over the years but was used again in the First World War to mill flour, finally ceasing operation in 1919. The mill is built at the highest point on Sark, 356 feet above sea level, and, because of its vantage point, was used as a look out by German forces in World War Two when the two remaining sails and the roof were dismantled. Some of the gear from the sails can still be seen on the ground below the tower. Between 2003 and 2004 the interior was refurbished by Richard Axton and Jeremy la Trobe Bateman. After the mill walk down the hill and round the bend to find the Visitor Centre on your right.

≈⊙≈ Walk Seven ⊙≈
Dixcart Valley

This walk through Dixcart Valley to the beach takes about one hour and fifteen minutes. There are two rather steep ascents. The route is at its best in spring when the bluebells are out. It is also a sheltered walk if the wind has settled in to the north or north east. It starts and ends at La Collinette.

Walk south leaving the Nat West Bank on your right. Take the second turning on your right and proceed along a wide track with a tennis court over the bank on your right. Ignore all left and right turns until you pass some conifers on your left. At the next junction, bear right passing more conifers on your left and begin the descent in to the valley. There are good views over towards Jersey on the left. After passing a small quarry on your right walk down a wide track with trees on each side. Take the first left turn, just before you reach the staff building of Stocks Hotel and walk down this narrower path which is particularly beautiful when the bluebells are out.

The well at Petit Dixcart

As you walk down the valley with the stream on your right you will notice that trees have been felled and others tidied up or new ones planted. Dixcart Valley was badly hit by the 1987 October gale which did major damage in all the Channel Islands. At the next junction at the house called Petit Dixcart carry straight on signed 'Dixcart Bay'. Peep over the wall to admire the beautiful Jersey style farmhouse with its dower cottage. You will also pass a well on your left and it is interesting to note that there is no standard water supply on Sark. Each property owner is responsible for his or her own provision. Traditional wells are now utilised by electric pumps and the water is piped direct to the house. Other houses have bore holes and fortunately the island appears to have adequate aquifers (underground lakes) for our present requirements. Many islanders also collect, store and use catchment water.

Cross the bridge so that you now have the stream on your left. Continue descending the valley and, ignoring two paths on your right, go down the steps on to the beach taking care to heed the warning notice about falling rocks while you explore the bay with its beautiful arch of rock.

Dixcart Bay

Dixcart is probably Sark's most popular beach but even in high summer you can find plenty of space to sit and rest, read, simply enjoy the view or watch the activities of visiting boat crews as Dixcart is a popular anchorage.

Like many of the other flat beaches of the Channel Islands the surface of Dixcart can change with the action of winds and tides. Sometimes the whole bay is sandy while at other times it is predominantly pebbly. There is always hard flat sand at low tide though which makes that the best time for swimming though a reasonable 'dip' can be had at most states of the tide.

L'Étac

When you are ready to return, go back up the steps then take the first turning on the left. You will start to ascend quite steeply so take a break to admire the view. The large pyramid shaped rock, which is in fact an islet, is L'Étac. In late spring and early summer this is a breeding site for those clowns of the sea, the puffins, as well as razorbills, guillemots, gulls and shags. The best way to see these birds is by taking a round the island boat trip, a voyage which, when the tide allows, can also include close views of some of Sark's caves. Like the guillemots at Les Autelets (see walk four), puffins and razorbills only come ashore to breed with each pair raising a single chick. Razorbills favour a rocky ledge or sheltered crevice while puffins lay their egg in a burrow, either digging one for themselves or commandeering a rabbit hole. Around the middle of July the young birds leave their nest site and they and their parents head far away from land to spend the rest of year at sea.

Puffins

Razorbill

L'Étac is also one of the island's top sites for scuba diving. Its sheer rocky walls are exposed to the full force of the tide creating the perfect habitat for a wealth of marine life including a rich variety of fish, stunningly colourful anemones and several species of coral. Sark is a popular destination for divers although the strong currents around the off-shore reefs can prove quite a challenge for the novice. The island's southerly position means that some of the marine life here is rarely, if ever encountered further north. The chance of seeing these species and the clarity of the water make Sark particularly popular with marine biologists and underwater photographers.

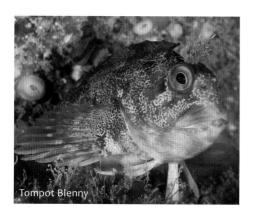
Tompot Blenny

Fan Coral

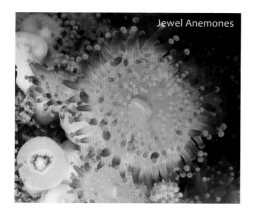
Jewel Anemones

Cuckoo Wrasse

Anemone Prawn

Sunset Cup Coral

If the day is hot and the ascent tiring you will find two benches about two thirds up this path, an even better place to admire the views. The path gradually flattens out and if you are sharp eyed you may notice, on your right, a tiny oak tree singled out for special attention with protective chicken wire with a small plaque. During the second world war British commandos raided all of the Channel Islands which were, at the time, occupied by forces of the German army. In October 1942 there was a Commando raid in the Dixcart area, code named Operation Basalt, which had far reaching effects in other parts of the world. The leader of the raiding party was Major John Geoffrey Appleyard who died later in the war at Monte Cassino. The tiny oak commemorates his life and was brought from Italy in 2009. The story of Operation Basalt is an interesting one and further details can be found at the Visitor Centre which you will pass later in the walk.

Le Manoir

Part of the de Carteret coat of arms

The track widens and at the next junction bear left and proceed along this path with open fields on each side. At the field gate with the stile do not go over the stile or through the gate but bear right then left, descending to Dixcart Hotel which will be on your right. At the junction by Stocks Hotel, a little further on bear right then immediately left on to new cobbles passing the hotel on your left and the staff accommodation on your right. Walk straight on with meadows on each side.

At the junction with the road stop to admire Le Manoir. This was the original home of the early Seigneurs and is a Jersey style farmhouse. Really sharp eyed walkers may notice the diamonds of the de Carteret coat of arms in the stone work on the left of the main roof.

Sark Visitor Centre

Bear right on the road. Just after the bend you will notice the building that used to be the girls' school and then the junior school. With the completion of the new school in 2005 this building became available and is now the Visitor Centre and the headquarters of La Societe Sercquaise, Sark's local history and natural history society. Both are well worth a visit and have exhibitions through the spring, summer and autumn. The Visitor Centre, which is staffed throughout the day in the season, is also a good source of maps and booklets which can enhance your stay in Sark.

Sark Prison

Next to the Visitor Centre is Sark's tiny prison. This has two cells and a lavatory. It is not usually open to visitors because it is still very occasionally used, though Sark's crime rate, as you can imagine, is low!

Just after the gate in to the Visitor Centre bear right and proceed along the Avenue to return to La Collinette.

The Avenue

Hotel

The Avenue

La Collenette

Bel Air Inn

Harbour Hill

95

90

85

80

La Forge

75

Gu

Le Petit Dixcart

60

Creux du Derrible

Pe D Ba

Derrib Headla

Hogsback

Gun

Derrible Bay

Derrible Point

Point Château

Copyright © States of Guernsey 2011

Walk Eight
Hogsback & Derrible

This walk, which starts and ends at the Collinette takes about an hour and fifteen minutes. It is rather more demanding than most of the other strolls and there is a fair amount of change of level and some steps. There is also the option of descending to explore Derrible Bay. This would increase the time required by at least one hour but is well worth the detour.

Derrible Bay

Start at the Collinette proceeding south, leaving the Nat West Bank on your right. Follow the main road bearing left where it forks. At an attractive small stone house, La Peigneurie, turn right, signed 'Dixcart Bay'. Continue down the track with a white house on your right. When you reach a three way junction, bear left, signed 'Hog's Back'. Walk between two field gates along a wide grassy track noticing distant views on your right over Little Sark.

La Peigneurie

Blackthorn blossom

Sloes

The path narrows and, in spring you are surrounded by the confetti-like blossom of the blackthorn. Sloes, the fruit of these thorny plants, are harvested by locals, as well as a few sloe pirates from Guernsey and Jersey, in October and many families will offer guests a nip of local sloe gin after a meal. An easy to remember recipe is one third of sloes (pricked), one third of gin, one third of sugar. Leave from October until at least Christmas, turning occasionally to spread the sugar. Strain off the sloes before drinking. There are many variations on the basic recipe and the sloe gin category is hotly contested in Sark's Midsummer Garden and Farm Produce Show.

Cannon on the Hog's Back

At the next junction carry straight on enjoying wide sea vistas on each side. Continue to the end of the spine of the Hog's Back where you will find a cannon, this one unmounted. Dixcart Bay is on your right and Derrible on your left. L'Étac, an offshore islet which is home to puffins (see walk seven) is ahead in the distance. The end of the Hog's Back is, in my opinion, one of the best 'top of the world' picnic spots but you may care to have a thought for the commandos of Operation Basalt (see walk seven) who ascended the cliff from sea level here on a misty night in October 1942, when much of Sark was mined.

Oxeye Daisies on the Hog's Back with Derrible Bay beyond

Retrace your steps to the first junction and this time follow the path on your right. You will now encounter some changes of level but the path is sound and has steps where necessary. There are quite a few young deciduous trees along this path which were planted as part of an island scheme in the 1990s. Pass through a gate which crosses the path and keep ascending. At the top of the path, skirt the field towards a bench which you may well appreciate as perhaps it is time for a rest and also it is at this point that you need to decide whether or not to embark on the steep descent to Derrible Bay. If you do, continue a little further and follow the sign 'Derrible Bay'. The path, which though steep is quite well made, zig zags all the way down to the beach.

The path to the Hog's Back & Derrible Bay

Derrible Beach

Derrible Bay is one of the most spectacular in Sark and is best explored at or near low tide when the swimming is at its best. A vast expanse of flat, hard sand is exposed and, at the top of the bay, there are caves which are easy to explore. You can also go in to the huge collapsed cave which is known as Creux Derrible. It is worth remembering that the stony area at the top of the bay, where most people choose to sit, is cut off from the access to the bottom of the steps as the tide comes in.

The main walk continues from the bench which you passed right up at the top. Follow a dip in the field and then proceed through two gates, passing a dew pond on your left, to get back to the road. The second gate has sign posts 'Derrible Bay, Hogs Back and Les Laches'. When you reach the road turn left and continue on it until it bends back to La Collinette.

✎ Walking in Little Sark ✎

A visit to Sark is not complete without a trip to Little Sark, particularly for those who love walking. Biking or strolling out there can be something of an adventure in itself. As you walk, or push your bike across the narrow isthmus of La Coupée, consider what it must have been like to do this before the railings were in place.

The two walks described here can be joined to make one longer one. The first is shown in the red, the second in pink. Little Sark is farmed and there may be sheep, cattle or horses in some fields. Several of the paths mentioned are quite near the edge so reasonable caution must be taken and any gates opened need to be closed behind you. There are also a number of stiles and these can be a little slippery if conditions are wet.

The paths of Sark are not busy and those on Little Sark are even less so. You may see no other walkers at all and much of the time you will only hear natural sounds: the waves, the birds, the baaing of sheep and, on occasions in the middle of a hot day, absolutely nothing at all.

The ruins of Little Sark's Mill

◈ Walk Nine ◈
Little Sark West

The walk, which starts at La Sablonnerie Hotel, takes about an hour and fifteen minutes, allowing a little time for detours on to promontories to admire spectacular views. The terrain is varied and includes some stiles and a small amount of change of level. In the area of the ruined buildings of the silver mines it is important to stay on the paths.

La Duvallerie Farm

At the corner by the Sablonnerie Hotel do not bear left but carry straight on with your back to the hotel. Walk a short distance along this road with cottages on your left and a house on your right until you reach a farmyard with a traditional stone farmhouse.

Just before the farmhouse, turn right in to a field, which may have stock or horses in it. Skirt this field on the left next to a gorse bank as if you are walking down towards the substantial stone house ahead of you. Along the bank, you will come to the ruins of a building on your left. Here you turn left going through the gap in the bank and then through a gate. Go across the next field to the gap in the next bank. Go through this gap in to the next field skirting a fence on your left and admiring views over Brecqhou and the Pilcher Monument to your right. Cross the stile on your left. Skirt the field on the seaward side and as the field narrows look for a stile between the bank and the seaward side. Cross the stile and bear right then left to enjoy spectacular views over Brecqhou on the right, Herm, Jethou and Guernsey in the distance ahead and a large rock called Bretagne below. This is a good picnic spot.

Bretagne

Gorse

To return to the main path from this headland face the long finger-like obelisk of the Pilcher Monument in the distance on Big Sark and follow the grassy track bearing right to carefully continue along the edge of the cliff keeping to the higher level as much as possible. Continue to the stile which you cross. Skirt the field keeping on the right until you reach another stile. Cross this one on to a grassy path which meanders between the gorse, at its best in early spring when it scents the air with its heady coconut fragrance.

At the junction in the path branch right to walk on to a promontory which gives views over Port Gorey and is another great picnic spot or keep straight on to continue the walk. In winter, you may notice the white 'tents' of the brown-tail moth or their rather lighter summer versions in the blackthorn. Periodic explosions of these moths occur and when the species become abundant allergic reactions to the airborne hairs can be suffered by some people. Some years ago during one such explosion the people of Sark formed work groups to cut out and burn the 'tents' in March before the caterpillars emerged. Pheromone traps have also been utilised and you may glimpse one of these, looking rather like a white milk carton, in the bushes. (If you see one, please leave it where it is.)

Brown-tail moth tent

Port Gorey

The path bends around eventually coming out above Port Gorey. In 1833 silver and copper lodes were identified at Le Pot on the east of Little Sark. These proved disappointing to the mining operation that was set up but in 1836 silver- lead ore was found at Port Gorey. Four shafts were sunk, the deepest to six hundred feet. Two steam engines were located, one to pump out water and the other to raise and lower cages. About two hundred and fifty miners came in, mainly from Cornwall and seventy or eighty local people were employed too. The then Seigneur, Ernest Le Pelley, invested heavily in to the mining company but in 1845 the ceiling of the lowest gallery collapsed and the workings were flooded. In 1847 all work ceased and the bonanza, which never produced much silver, was over. Ernest Le Pelley had not only lost money but had mortgaged many properties and on his death, his son Pierre was forced to seek Crown permission to sell the Fief of Sark. It was bought by Marie Allaire, widow of Mr T G Collings, for the sum of £6000 less £4000 already advanced as a mortgage and £616.13.4 overdue interest. This is how the Collings family, ancestors of the present Seigneur John Michael Beaumont, came to hold the Fief of Sark.

Remains of the silver mine buildings

As you over look and descend in to the valley you will see the ruins of supports of the winding gear, chimneys, a building that was probably an overseer's office. Other buildings can be seen as can spoil heaps and the route of a tram cart system if you descend down to the sea.

Returning to the present time and the walk: cross the next stile and start your descent to yet another stile and steps down in to the valley. At the junction turn left to ascend by a wide path and some shallow steps to a gate where you join the road and turn left to return to La Sablonnerie Hotel. Alternatively, to join walk ten, cross diagonally at this junction and follow that path. If you wish to explore other relics of the mining boom bear right down to the sea before returning.

∼ Walk Ten ∼
Little Sark South East

This very gentle walk takes about half an hour and starts from La Sablonnerie. It could be viewed as an after lunch or before dinner stroll. As with stroll nine, some of the route is quite close to the edge of the cliff.

Venus Pool

At La Sablonnerie turn left and walk down the road which starts with the hotel on your left and the tea gardens on your right, passing cottages where you keep left at the bend following the wooden sign which says 'Silver Mine and Venus Pool'. Continue on this road until you come to a gate on your right signed 'Silver Mine and Venus Pool'. Go through the gate and down shallow steps and a wide grassy path until you come to a junction where there are three options. Take the left path and continue on this, ignoring a left turn into a field. Proceed along the wide grassy path passing a small section of wooden railings on your right. As you ascend views over Jersey in the distance enable you to look across to St Ouen's Bay and Corbiere Lighthouse on that island. The path opens out and becomes less obvious but be reassured by a bench on your left.

Just after this bench you need to branch left. The famed Venus Pool or Venus Bath is off to your right and is accessed by starting on the path on the right just after the bench. This path goes down to two cairns and after these it is a scramble, following a very faint path to the right and then a natural yellowish line in the rock to the left. The large rock pool, in which you can swim, is only uncovered for about two hours either side of low water. Sadly, it cannot be seen from above.

The Venus Pool is the subject of an oil painting by the Victorian Artist William Toplis. He visited Sark in 1883 on holiday and remained on the island for a further 60 years painting many land and seascapes in a detailed and sometimes enigmatic fashion. Reproductions of his pictures, and more information about the painter, can be seen in the Toplis Room at the Island Hall.

Dolmen

Having branched left after the bench continue with gorse bushes on both sides. If you are sharp eyed, you may spot a small dolmen in the distance along the coast to your left. This is believed to be 4,000 years old and is Sark's only complete dolmen. A huge capstone is supported by five of the ten boulders below to form a simple cist.

At the junction carry straight on passing close by a stone chimney on your left where there is also a bench looking out to sea. Where the path joins the road turn left to return to La Sablonnerie Hotel.

Silver mine chimney

◈ Walk Eleven ◈
Sark in the Dark

This little book would not be complete without offering the reader an opportunity to experience a walk in the dark. We have no cars and no street lights. Tractors, apart from emergency vehicles, are not allowed on the roads between 10pm and 6am though you may encounter the double lamps of a carriage bringing someone home from a late night supper.

In January 2011 Sark was designated the world's first Dark Sky Island by the International Dark-sky Association (IDA) This was for the quality of our night sky, the lack of light pollution and the mission statement of the island to keep it that way. The best time to watch stars and planets is when there is no, or very little, moonlight and before you start your walk you may wish to have a look at various sources that give information on the celestial happenings (www.nightskyinfo.com is one possibility but your search engine will give you many options) or you may choose to simply gaze in wonderment at the millions of heavenly bodies.

You may, of course, prefer a moonlit night. There is little that is more romantic than gazing over the sea with a beam of moonlight stretching across it. Constellations which can be seen and phases of the moon change from night to night. The constancy of reliable lighthouses and other navigation aids with lights are just the opposite, remaining on station and confirming to mariners land they may want to approach or hazards they may need to avoid. Lighthouses and other marine lights give out different signals to identify themselves and even with the advent of sophisticated electronic navigating devices most mariners welcome the confirmation of location that a lighthouse or lightbuoy can give them.

Choose a still, clear night. A torch is an obvious necessity and perhaps a spare, just in case. If you are walking alone, it is a good idea to tell someone where you are going. Above all, enjoy this very special walk which gives you the rare opportunity to stroll safely at night to identify some of the lights around Sark's coast and the adjacent islands and coast of France as well as simply appreciating the night sky.

Stars above Point Robert Lighthouse

Star trails over the north coast

This walk takes about one hour and forty-five minutes allowing plenty of time to stop and gaze. It starts and ends at the Collinette and includes parts of some of the day time walks. It is easy walking, mainly on the flat, but remember, it really is dark!

Head north leaving HSBC Bank on your right. Take the first turning on the right. Continue on this road until you can look through a gap between two modern houses on your right. In the distance you should see three red lights arranged vertically. These are on the television mast in Jersey. To the right of this, low down in the sea, you should see the nine quick flashes of the Desormes Buoy which warns shipping to keep to the west of the dangerous Banc Desormes off the north west coast of Jersey. Looking further in to the distance you may spot the loom of Corbiere Lighthouse off the south west coast of that island. The channel of sea between Jersey and Sark is called the Deroute and is well used by shipping heading between France and England. If you see a vessel that is very well lit and moving slowly, it may be a cruise liner. The ferry between Portsmouth and St Malo also passes that way and it is also a popular fishing ground so you may see smaller vessels carrying their compulsory lights which identify their size and direction of travel.

Continue along this road until you come to a gap in the bank. Pause here and look out to sea. You should see the three quick flashes of the Blanchard Buoy which alerts shipping to the presence of the Blanchard Bank, a popular fishing ground with locals but a danger to the unwary. Further in the distance you should see the very strong signal of Cape Carteret Lighthouse in Normandy. Its signal, two plus one flashes every 15 seconds, can be seen from 26 miles away.

After the gap in the hedge, bear left and carry straight on, ignoring the right turn. At the next junction carry straight on for a short while then take a right turn and descend the hill. This is a very dark area and a good point to stand still, turn off your torch and have your first gaze upwards to see how many constellations and planets you can identify.

At the bottom of the hill, turn left then almost immediately right, ascending a concrete road up to Point Robert Lighthouse. Shortly you will be standing directly above Point Robert Lighthouse. Now automatic, this lighthouse is administered by Trinity House and can be seen from 20 miles by vessels approaching the island. In the distance to the north and north west flashes of lighthouses on Cap de la Hague in France and on Alderney can often be seen. To the east the lights on the French coast are clearly visible.

The next section of the walk is an off road dark experience but if you have already done walk two then you have tried it in the light. Bear left just before the wall and skirt the field until you come to a gap. Continue with the hedge on your right until you reach a narrow gap with a stone stile. While you are doing this, you may be surprised by the rather eerie experience of having the beam of Point Robert Light sweeping the sea along aside where you are walking. Go over the stile and proceed diagonally across the field. Follow the path on the right around the cliff but go through a small gate on your left about 50 metres before the end of the path then follow the path through the middle of two small fields. Where the field joins the road, turn right but do not descend down the field to Greve de la Ville follow the road as it winds around passing between a farm house and a small cottage. At the next junction turn left signed 'village' and at the junction after that turn right.

Though you are now on one of Sark's main roads the general area is very dark so this is another opportunity to gaze up at the night sky. In addition to stars and planets you may see a moving sputnik still orbiting the earth since its launch many years ago or an aeroplane. This is also near one of the island's several bat roosts so you may encounter these little creatures whizzing about. Despite rapid changes of direction and high speeds their sonar will ensure that they do not fly in to you. The area is not only dark but also pretty quiet so, as your sense of sight is restricted, what can you hear? Perhaps the distant call of an oystercatcher disturbed from its roost, the exotic 'churr' of the great green bush-cricket, the church bells or the low engine noise of one of the fast catamarans that travel between the Channel Islands, the UK and France? A black rat may cross your path. The only species of rat in Sark,

Stars above St Peter's Church

Star trails over the Burons with the lights of France beyond

it is now one of the rarest mammals in the British Isles. Perhaps your sense of smell may also be enhanced? My favourite night smell is that of the elaeagnus shrub which is a very common edging to Sark roads and seems to perfume the night air.

After the S bends, bear left at the next junction. You are now walking across the top of the island and this is another good area for star watching. At the junction, turn right, signed 'L'Eperquerie and Shooting Range'. Where the road runs out, turn left on to a grassy footpath by a litter bin. At the very end of the Eperquerie Common there is a small red/white light, the original of which was given to the island by the La Trobe Bateman family. This warns mariners away from the hazards around our north coast. Until very recently, when a new light was fitted, Jeremy la Trobe-Bateman occasionally had to clamber out to the very end of the point bearing a car battery to operate the light if the solar energy, its usual power source, was insufficient. It is fortunate that all La Trobe-Batemans, like their ancestors who wrote the famous La Trobe guide to the 'Coast, Caves and Bays of Sark', are prodigious rock scramblers!

After about 200 metres the path bears right but you need to find a bench on your left at this point so that you can sit down to admire the lights on the neighbouring islands and off lying rocks. Brecqhou is on your left, and you are facing Jethou and Herm with Guernsey behind them. A large amount of rocks extends to the north and south of Herm and Jethou. There are passages through but the route for large commercial shipping is south of the Lower Heads buoy which gives six quick flashes every 15 seconds. In front of Herm you may see the signal mast on the Noire Pute rock which flashes white and red every fifteen seconds and, in front of Jethou, the buoy which is north of the Fourquies reef which flashes continuously.

On the south coast of Guernsey you may see the three flashes of the light on St Martin's Point and, if you have very good eyesight, the alternate red and white flashes of the light on the south arm of St Peter Port Harbour, below Castle Cornet.

However, you may not wish to concentrate on all this at all but just sit and enjoy the peace of night time Sark. When you are ready to make a move retrace your steps to the road and then turn right and go back to the junction with the sign. Carry straight on past the Seigneurie gates and then on to the crossroad which are just after the Island Hall. At this crossroad, turn left and enjoy your final good star watching site as you walk down this road. At the next crossroad turn right to return to the Collinette.

(The images of star trails are created with a one hour exposure revealing the rotation of the earth while the pole star remains static.)

Stars above the Seigneurie dovecote

Honeysuckle

Bell Heather

Sea Campion

Sheep's Bit

Common Dog-violet

Thrift

Scentless Mayweed & Corn Marigold

Red Campion

Blackthorn

Rock Sea-spurrey

Sand Crocus

Common Knapweed

Stork's-bill

Wild Garlic

Autumn Squill

English Stonecrop

Giant Butterbur

Ivy-leaved Toadflax

Wild Thyme

Portland Spurge

✍ Acknowledgements ✍

Many have helped, advised and encouraged in the writing and production of this book and we are grateful for all the help. Particularly we would like to thank:

• The landowners of Sark who allow access over their land and make strolling such a wonderful experience on our island.

• Eugene and Edric who tend the paths, thoroughly and with love, allowing us to enjoy the wildflowers as well as the views.

• Philip who knows everything that there is to know about Little Sark and was happy to share this information with us.

• William and Annabel who cut back their path above the Port du Moulin allowing us the best view of guillemots in the Channel Islands.

• Darryl Ogier, Karpal Chana and Dave Killan who assisted us in our search for a base map with contours.

• Kate and Jenny who tested walks and Kate who proof read.

• Anna who allowed us to use one of her beautiful paintings of Sark.

• Small Island Publishing who allowed the idea of this project to become a reality.

La Grande Grève by Anna Le Moine Gray